PROMOTE!

. . .

PROMOTE!

It's Who Knows What You Know That Makes a Career

Professionally Promote Yourself to the Top

Rick Gillis

Guest Introduction by Dayna Steele

Edited by Ronni Bennett

Cover Art &
Design: Gargi Kundu
Cover Photo: Alisa Murray

For more information, to obtain a media bio or to contact Rick Gillis
visit www.rickgillis.com

Accomplishments | Advancement | Assessment
Branding | Business Management | Career | Employment |
Engagement
Personal Growth | Promotion

\\\

ISBN: 1507632355
ISBN 13: 9781507632352
Library of Congress Control Number: 2015900887
CreateSpace Independent Publishing Platform
North Charleston, South Carolina

Books by Rick Gillis

JOB!
Learn How to Find Your Next Job in One Day

The Real Secret to Finding a Job?
Make Me Money or Save Me Money!

Make Me Money or Save Me Money!
The Real Secret to Finding a Job
for New and Recent College Graduates

Really Useful Job Search Tactics
A Handbook of Contemporary Job Hunting Techniques

Promote   verb   prə-ˈmōt
To change the rank or position of (someone) to a higher or more important one (advancement)
Synonym: Advance, Further, Elevate

"Be yourself, everyone else is already taken."
Oscar Wilde

*"Never assume that anyone,
even your immediate supervisor,
knows exactly what you do."*
Rick Gillis

*"Those who say it cannot be done
should get out of the way of those doing it."*
Chinese Proverb

Mary

. . .

Table of Contents

Foreword

Dayna Steele

No matter what profession you are in (or want to be in) and where you are at any given moment in your success journey, you must be able to articulate your value to an organization, management, clients, even your own personal network of friends and family. You have the ability to get everything you want as long as you work smart *and* learn how to professionally let everyone know your value.

Rick and I agree it is your professional responsibility to make sure that those who hold the key to your success, such as supervisors and managers, know the value you bring to the job every day. They have to know how important you are. This is not bragging - if you learn to do it correctly. This is nothing more than informing your way to the top and Rick will show you how in this book.

I have met and worked with some of the greatest rock stars, and now business stars, in the world. You may see the end results of all their efforts and be thinking 'I wish I had that life.' Know that every one of those rock/business stars had to work just as hard at promoting themselves as they did at excelling at their craft and performance. Before the managers and limos there was self-promotion. And, self-promotion is something that never stops – if you want to succeed. What are you doing today, right now, to advance your career in the eyes of those who can make a difference?

PROMOTE! may be one of the most significant books you will ever read. It's that important. Personal promotion is something you must learn to get to the top and keep doing to stay there.

Dayna Steele
Speaker, CEO, YourDailySuccessTip.com & Author
The "101 Ways to Rock Your World" book series and "Rock to the Top"

Introduction

As I was writing PROMOTE! I got to thinking about how much more I might have achieved in my corporate commercial real estate career (what I did prior to the job board/job search business) had I recognized at the time that professionally I was *at the mercy of my supervisors.* To be candid, I did pretty well, but I now wonder how much more I could have accomplished had I known then what you will soon be learning. Looking back I now know that I missed opportunities for advancement by not being prepared to speak up on my own behalf.

As a nationally recognized career coach I have spent thousands of hours working with individuals across the nation. One of the commonplace factors that I came to recognize among clients was how very few of them were capable of expressing their commercial value. After a time I came to consider this a professional career deficiency.

PROMOTE! was written based on the insight gained from coaching as well as from personal experience. The concept is simple: Learn how to professionally promote yourself to those to whom you are professionally at the mercy of.

Inform your employers on a consistent basis that you deserve the chance, the raise, the promotion and the opportunity to be all that you are capable of being. It is your professional responsibility to yourself, as well as to your loved ones, to achieve all you can in the very short time you have allotted to you in this life.

I wish you great success!

Rick Gillis

Chapter 1

40 YEARS

Farmers say that they have 40 chances – that is, roughly 40 years in a working lifetime, to bring in the crops.

You probably aren't a farmer but you have about the same number of years to bring in your own "crops." By that I mean reaching the level of achievement most of us strive for: fulfilling work, personal satisfaction, professional achievement and recognition, good pay, a successful retirement if not outright wealth, raising a family and creating a legacy for children, grandchildren and more.

In short, pursuit of the dreams we all seek from life, the reasons we get out of bed every day throughout each year's seasons until, for whatever reason, we are done. We get about 40 years to do that and how we put those 40 years to use in the workplace is crucial to the outcome.

Before I go any further it is important for you to know that, until recently, I was in the business of job search coaching. I am particularly proud of those job search techniques and products I created for the benefit of my clients and, by extension, the public. (See About the Author at the back of the book.) It is one of these unique products, the Accomplishments Statement, that this book is based on.

During my years of teaching people how to find good jobs, I also developed a new kind of resume that, in place of the traditional jobs-listed-in-chronological-order format, is based on accomplishments. Here's why. Most resumes are little more than obituaries — they speak to the past when what every employer *really* wants to know is how you will impact their future: what you're going to accomplish for him or her if you are hired.

Such a resume, based on solid accomplishments, requires a different format, a different verb tense, even a different voice and it remains a highly successful format for thousands of job seekers.

However, as effective as that resume has been, my many years of working with job seekers revealed a common shortcoming among them. Whether a recent graduate looking for that first job or an executive seeking a new opportunity, when confronted with a formal interview frequently they shared an inability to express their value in a way that would wow their audience, be that a shop foreman or a board of directors.

Question: *What do celebrities have in common with annual reports?*
Answer: *Both have a publicity machine behind them.*

Every major personality you have ever admired has professional management; a team of experts choreographing their every move who then have their client's affairs reported to you as "news." So too does every product you buy, every holding in your portfolio, have its own team of experts promoting their 'client.' Whether through internal marketing or advertising or by way of an outside public relations firm, these experts are tasked with doing everything in their power to be sure you and I know only the best about their client.

Who do you have?

You only have YOU.

And that's what this book is all about: You. How you can, and must in today's employment world and into the future, become your own publicity machine.

It's about how you can toot your own horn on the job, promote yourself without being obnoxious and convince your employer of your value so that you can make every one of those 40 years of work as gratifying, productive and successful as possible.

While on the subject, let me provide you with the best definition of personal promotion and professional engagement you will ever hear:

It's not who you know.
It's not even what you know.
It's who knows what you know that makes a career.

Chapter 2

Are You Valuable?

Are you valuable? Of course you are!

When I ask this question in my presentations, I don't move on until I hear it from everyone in the room loud and clear and with conviction: "Yes! I am valuable!"

Cheesy? Maybe so. The point I'm trying to impress on the audience is that we are all valuable but rarely, if ever, do we take the time to make it personal — to ourselves and especially to those who hold our future in their hands: our supervisors.

Mostly, we wait until someone else slaps us on the back and then, in an "aw shucks" moment, we reluctantly accept the praise with a little bow of the head while figuratively digging our toe into the dirt.

But that's not good enough.

**"It is your professional responsibility
to make decision makers aware of the value
you bring to the organization."**

That's right; it is your *professional responsibility* to promote yourself to your company. Remember the 40 years or so that you have to create your legacy? And in my introduction where I wondered aloud how much better my own real estate career might have been had I been taught what I'm sharing with you right now? No matter where you might be on your current career path, *now* is the time to professionally promote yourself. Tomorrow is too late.

THE REAL WORLD

Let's briefly talk about the hard knocks of life and work. In the real world you are at the mercy of those who supervise you. That is how it will always be unless you become self-employed.

In the course of your career you may have attended or will attend conferences where the company CEO will rouse and motivate all in attendance with his glowing vision for the future. And the future is bright indeed—for all but one who never saw it coming.

Immediately following this rallying of the troops our CEO is being escorted back to his car by the Senior Vice President who only an hour earlier had enthusiastically introduced him to the conference. Turning to his SVP the CEO abruptly informs him that the board met and he has been let go—his services are no longer needed by the company.

As brutal as this account may sound, it happens every day. All too often the reason an employee finds him or herself on the losing end of such an encounter is because he or she had not *consistently* communicated their value to management regardless of how close they might have been to their immediate supervisor.

Let me say it again: It is as much your *professional responsibility* to promote yourself as it is for you to perform to your highest capabilities on the job.

I vividly recall the first time I mentioned this phrase, *professional responsibility*, to a live audience. There was a slight pause from the 300 or so people in the room as they recognized the power in this statement.

There was a collective affirmation as they recognized I was giving them 'permission' to do something they had never been permitted to do before. I was granting them the permission to *professionally promote themselves*.

•   •   •

If you are not comfortable *with the terms 'boasting,' or 'promoting' perhaps you should think of it as 'informing' others of your value.*

• • •

From the time we are kids, we are taught (properly, I might add) that bragging about ourselves is inappropriate. Better to let others discover on their own how wonderful we are.

Well, here's the problem: they probably won't.

It is my opinion that by the time young people enter high school they should be taught by parents, teachers, coaches and mentors how to *appropriately* express their value to the team, to the class, to the environment and to themselves. And I say this in particular for girls.

I don't pretend to have all the answers as to how women will finally, *truly* break through the glass ceiling—at least in the aspect that is most easily measured: Equal pay for equal work—but I know the time is coming soon. What I will say is that this book and the idea of timely, appropriate, professional and continuous self-promotion on the job is one of those tools that women must learn and confidently apply in the workplace.

• • •

Remember those celebrities in the last chapter? Musicians, actors, athletes, even politicians, didn't get where they are without banging their own drums until they found enough success to hire PR experts to do it for them. They knew they couldn't make a dent in their chosen field until they got noticed so they made it their job, their *professional responsibility* to promote themselves until someone else took notice.

"Someone else" like, maybe, your boss. But it is unlikely to happen unless and until you promote yourself. Why not stack the odds in your favor?

EMPLOYEE MISTAKE #1
"Never assume that anyone,
even your immediate supervisor,
knows exactly what you do."

This assumption can be a ruinous professional mistake. It doesn't matter if your boss is in Tulsa or across the hall, if you share a cubicle or you report virtually to the corporate offices in London. Whether the distance between you is 6,000 miles or 60 feet, it is unlikely that your boss knows much more about what you do than the minimum she expects from you.

For the sake of discussion, let's say you work on the same floor as your immediate supervisor. Your environment allows you to see each other frequently. You pass in the hall and come together at staff meetings. With such proximity, it's easy to believe he or she knows all about you and your talents. Wrong.

9

"Just because you share air at the office does not make you item number one in your boss's mind."

Believe it or not, he or she has responsibilities other than you. They include, for example, 15 other people who may be managed on site or virtually, inventory to deal with, new software to be selected, implemented, tweaked and rolled out to the department or companywide.

And then there is a regional quarterly meeting to prepare for and, oh yeah, that big presentation early next week that needs to be fine-tuned in the anticipation of acquiring a major new account.

And you think your boss knows how you contribute to the overall mission? Not necessarily.

"Make sure decision makers are continuously aware of the value you bring to the organization."

Your boss may have a general idea about what you do and how that makes an impact on some of what she is working on but don't count on your supervisor clearly knowing the detail and specifics that you bring to the company. So...

"You already know how to dress to impress. It's time you learned how to express to impress."

Here's a trick question: What single word appears in all four of the quotes in this chapter? The answer is YOU. That's by design. This book is about you.

The repetition is important to remind YOU that is it YOU who must be doing the promoting of YOU. No one else is going to actively promote YOU.

If the idea of talking up your knowledge, talents and accomplishments makes you uncomfortable, makes you think that you're singing your own praises at the expense of the team, get over it because being too modest is not good for your career, for your pocketbook or for the company.

• • •

TYPE B PERSONALITIES AND PERSONAL PROMOTION

Over the years, I have worked with many highly skilled Type B personalities. People I call "Analyticals." Generally, but not exclusively, Analyticals come in three varieties: Information technology professionals, engineers or accountants—people who deal in absolute truths. As I describe it: To an engineer (most often a classic Type B) 1 + 1 will always = 2. Always. To a Type A personality salesperson, 1 + 1 will equal whatever it needs to be in order to seal the deal.

An Analytical, preferring to let their work speak for them, may have a difficult time speaking to their value. This can be a mistake. I prompt those Analyticals I have worked with to embrace my accomplishments mindset. In terms of confidence and poise the results have been remarkable.

• • •

If you are not regularly declaring your value to your boss, or your boss's boss, you may be in danger of losing your position because you can be certain someone else, potentially one of your own team members, is proclaiming his or her value.

Recently, a colleague mentioned to me that she had never promoted someone she didn't like. The question then becomes how does she come to prefer one employee over another? All things being equal, the answer lies in the ability of the chosen one to properly promote herself.

At first, it may feel like you are boasting and you are. But in today's lean, mean, highly efficient, social media savvy workplace environment, that's not just okay, it is mandatory for survival—when done properly.

At any moment you should be prepared to express how you are adding or added value to the organization today, yesterday, three days ago, three weeks ago, three months ago, last year and *what you will deliver in the future*. That's hard to do and I'm willing to bet you can't. Not yet anyway.

You might be thinking you can't be that precise. But that's where you are wrong. It's not that hard—once you establish the mindset and work the very simple plan that follows.

As I think you have gotten by now, I'm here to show you how to appraise your own performance and accomplishments so that you can state categorically that you are an indispensable member of the organization.

Chapter 3

Your New Professional Mindset

ACCOMPLISHMENT noun ə-käm-plish-mənt
- **Something done or achieved successfully (ACHIEVEMENT)**
- **The successful completion of something: the act of accomplishing something (COMPLETION)**

For the purposes of this book, let's expand that definition a little. An accomplishment is "The successful completion of something you did that you are proud of." It is something that prompts you to walk the walk and hold your head up a little higher around the workplace.

The trick to convincing your employer of your indispensability is having at your fingertips an inventory of real-world, on-the-job accomplishments that demonstrate your *commercial value* to the organization.

Commercial value? That might be a new concept to you but in fact every one you will ever work for will see you first as a commodity and secondly as a person. Sorry. Just being honest. Everything we will be discussing going forward with the exception of some entry-level stuff will be based on the commercial value of your efforts. During this process there will come a time and place to address volunteer and charity involvement but for the most part 'commercial' is where we will live for the remainder of this book.

Let me assure you that this commercial value aspect applies to every reader of this book no matter your position in the company. From entry-level to senior management, you must be able to express your value to those you report to.

> **"Never assume that anyone,**
> **even your immediate supervisor,**
> **knows exactly what you do."**

Think about your standing in the company this way: Remember how good you told them you were during the hiring process? Remember those interviews when you impressed even yourself with your spontaneity and amazing recall of previous successes? That result was due to your preparation for that specific event.

What if you had to re-apply for your current job every month? What would you say on a *monthly* basis that would convince your employer that you are an indispensable member of the team and worthy of being kept on the payroll? In today's world of work you must be able to make that distinction.

> **"Make sure decision makers
> are continuously aware of the value
> you bring to the organization."**
> *(Ideally without making enemies
> among your fellow workers)*

So how do you do that? This will surprise you: I don't know! Really. I don't.

Here's why: I don't know you. I don't know your personality. I don't know the culture of your company. I don't know your boss or the chemistry that exists (or doesn't) between him and you. I know nothing of the circumstances of your employment or the dynamics or politics that may be involved.

What I DO know is how to prepare you for the moment when the opportunity to make the case for how indispensable you are presents itself, and it's all about your specific accomplishments.

RESUMES ARE UNFAIR

First, some background on where this concept of PROMOTE! came from.

I believe that resumes are inherently unfair. In that short, little biographical document, an employer or recruiter is expected to read between the lines and determine that you are someone the organization wants to learn more about; someone to call to interview. In the not too distant past, hiring managers actually had time to read resumes but, as you know, technology intruded onto the landscape and due to the onslaught of resumes received for each position posted, resumes are given a short three to 10-second scan by a real human-person, and that is *after* the filtering software algorithm has spit out those resumes only a computer can love.

Knowing this, I came to realize that a resume is not enough; it alone will not do the job of getting anyone the attention they deserve—particularly at the interview. Simply stated, my job was to set my client candidates apart from the crowd so I created the Accomplishments Worksheet and Accomplishments Statement to give my clients an advantage over the competition in their job search.

Thereafter, when a hiring manager reviewed a resume followed by a formal, written statement of personal best accomplishments, the rate of success for my clients sky-rocketed. The Accomplishments Statement became the great equalizer that took a flat, lifeless list (what I would call a standard resume) and gave it the dynamics and voice necessary to make the hiring manager sit up and pay attention.

Why tell you all this? Because job seekers have often approached me thinking it was time for a change of scenery. They weren't getting ahead at their current job and they believed that a new employer would be the solution to the problem.

However, when we worked through my job search protocol of taking an accomplishments inventory, it often became clear that these candidates did not need a new environment where they would be more appreciated as much as they needed to take this personal accomplishments promotion concept to heart and apply it to their current situation. In several cases the idea of moving to a new company vanished as clients were able to obtain the recognition, promotion and financial compensation they sought at their current place of employment.

The Accomplishments Statement works equally well for those on the job.

This new component of your career tool kit will get you the promotion, the raise and, more importantly during hard times, the Accomplishments Statement can be the difference that keeps you on the payroll over another person who doesn't know how to effectively communicate his or her enduring value.

YOUR ACCOMPLISHMENTS AND 'INSIDER INFORMATION'

You view your paycheck as payment for the services you render and you are not incorrect. But your employer views your paycheck as his investment in you. And you know what happens to an investment (e.g., a stock) that is underperforming: It gets dumped.

But what if that investor had inside information that would indicate that she should hold on to that stock? Your accomplishments are that inside information. It is your responsibility to make certain your supervisor, your boss's boss and maybe even her boss's, boss's, boss has that information. Your value to the organization cannot travel high enough up the company hierarchy.

As you create your Accomplishments Statement, you will learn to assert your current and future value to an organization making yourself compelling and memorable to your present employer who in turn will recognize what sets you apart from your coworkers. This is what I like to call making personal promotion personal.

Now, before I show you how to create the document that will become more important to you over the 40 years of your career than your resume, take a look at the following sample Accomplishments Statement. You will want to refer to this document several times as we go forward. It is for that purpose that there is an identical copy available for quick access at the back of the book as well.

Janet Best
Statement of Professional Accomplishments
Giant Company, Inc. / Southeast US Regional VP

email@GiantCompanyWebsite.com   123.456.7890

- Completed special assignments on inventory phase-outs, unallocated materials, and obsolete inventory resulting in savings to the company of $1,500,000.

- Improved operation scores for district to 90% from 82% in prior years as a result of group and individual coaching of district front line employees.

- Delivered a 12% profit increase over prior regional management by establishing new institutional accounts resulting in $6,000,000 of new revenue.

- Successfully trained tri-state team of over 800 managers, sales reps, technicians, and support staff on key company programs which resulted in improving service levels by 10%, improved operations processes and increased customer satisfaction.

- Repair center team ranked No. 1 in the country by J.D. Power & Associates. Achieved this level of customer satisfaction with the active involvement of all team members contributing to the plan.

- Improved past due performance of vendors by implementing a daily expedite program. Result: Logistics performance improved 43% compared to past output; past due orders reduced to 6% within 5 months.

- Led nation with an 18% improvement of sales in electronics by training store personnel on educating the customer on product functionality and reliability.

- Performed annual performance reviews and facilitated employees' creation of individual development plans which led to increased employee satisfaction and motivation by 15% over previous management team.

- Managed direct reports of up to 40 associates which included hiring, training, evaluating, coaching and transitioning employees. Turnover rates decreased 34% over previous management team.

- Improved accuracy of $10,000,000 spare parts inventory by 11% within 6 months after initiating a cycle count program.

- Designed a new expediting procedure that resulted in increased customer satisfaction and on-time customer deliveries by 28% within 4 months.

Chapter 4

Think Quantification

I know what you're thinking: "What have I done that's going to amaze and impress my employer? I did not invent the iPhone, I'm not an expert in exchange-traded funds, I have not cured cancer and I can't prove the existence of the Loch Ness monster. So what makes *me* indispensable?"

Let me illustrate with a real-life story. When you finish reading it, you will never have to ask that question again.

The day I met Dave was one of the most profound experiences of my job search counseling days.

Dave was a payroll clerk looking for a payroll clerk job. To be candid, his resume was boring. I mean watching-paint-dry boring. Payroll clerk here, payroll clerk there—that was it. Dave and I huddled for 45 minutes while I coaxed and cajoled him to come up with at least ONE accomplishment that he was proud of. He could not think of anything he felt was worthy of mention but I was relentless, honestly, to the point of badgering.

Finally in exasperation, Dave dropped the bomb that the first payroll he had done for "Gigantic Global Energy Company" had involved 6,000 paychecks and that he had completed it alone, on time, with zero (ZERO!) returns.

Let's see: Thousands of paychecks representing countless pay rates and timesheets not to mention such details as overtime, vacation pay, sick days, taxes and withholding, and then there was the expectation that his clients, the company's employees, be paid accurately and on time. And he accomplished this while producing his first payroll at a brand new job. That is spectacular!

When I asked Dave why it had taken so long for him to come up with this extraordinary achievement, he simply said, "Because I was just doing what I was supposed to be doing."

And therein lies the lesson. Most of the time, your accomplishments are not earth shattering feats. Most of the time it is the stuff you do—and do well—as a normal, maybe even routine, part of your daily work. Think about that.

Many people, especially those who are not in sales, have trouble figuring out how they can quantify their value.

Think about the organization you work for. How many people do you think are actively involved daily in generating revenue? The correct answer is all of them—you included. But for the sake of illustration let's say it is just the sales team.

Except for sales-focused businesses like real estate and automobile sales, a majority of companies are comprised mostly of folks who support the sales function: front-end admin, manufacturing, service providers, inventory, shipping, billing, payroll, etc. You are a long way from alone in the business world if you think what you do does not generate revenue. And once again you would be wrong.

The fact that nothing happens until somebody sells something is accurate but once something is sold, it takes a lot of people working together to make the delivery. And generally nobody gets paid until the delivery is completed.

What this means is that most people don't sell but their services can still be quantified in dollars and percentages. To prove this I like to ask the question: How would an employer know what to pay you if your value could not be quantified?

QUANTIFYING YOUR VALUE

Let me explain. You were hired because someone believed you would produce more value for the organization than you would cost. There are only two ways that can be done: make them money or *save them* money and it is in this second regard that you do not have to be a bona fide revenue generator in order to be producing value for your company.

To be clear your pay includes not just your hourly wage plus taxes, social security and benefits (add about 30% for this—called burden—to your rate of pay) but also your part of the costs of equipment, hardware, software, phone systems, support staff, legal, inventory, facilities, utilities, advertising and marketing, printing, insurance, licenses, business taxes and so much more.

Every CEO and chief financial officer knows their operating cost down to the man-hour—that is, the average total cost to provide all the elements necessary for a company to perform their operations *per employee*, from the CEO to the shipping floor including the expenses listed above that have to be paid just to open the doors each day. If the business is not bringing in, *at minimum*, that much revenue plus a cushion called profit, they cannot continue to stay in business.

You remain valuable to a company, and therefore employed, *when your accomplishments continue to surpass your portion of the company's costs in you.*

Said another way, as long as the revenue determined to be generated by you exceeds the costs associated with employing you, you will remain on the job. Another point for your consideration is that the more you are paid the more value proportionally you are expected to deliver which, of course, makes sense.

A company can gamble on paying an entry-level employee $30,000 per year in the hopes that that person will quickly come up to speed and begin generating a respectable $45,000 or more in value. Such an employee would just pay for him- or herself with the employer taking the risk that with additional training and experience this staff member will increase their value to the company.

The same cannot be said of an employee earning $150,000 to $250,000 or more a year. Depending on the industry, this person must generate at least six to 10 times (ideally, more) their pay rate in order to be kept on staff. So if you have been with your company for a longer period of time, your ability to present factual accomplishments about your commercial value off the top of your head or in a formal statement is much more crucial than younger employees doing so simply because you earn more and are expected to return a proportionately larger return. AND, you need to be consistently informing the powers-that-be that you are doing so.

On a side note, go back to the beginning of that last paragraph and check out the dollar amounts. Did you notice that the zeros are 'spelled out?' This is by design and for impact. As much as possible 'spell out the zeros' when stating a dollar amount. $3.2 Million or $3.2MM is not nearly as attention grabbing as $3,200,000!

• • •

You should be familiar with the term Revenue per Employee or RPE. In 2013, for example, Apple's RPE for full-timers was $2,130,000 (!) according to the company's SEC Form 10K. Corporations know these numbers. You should too. Long term employees especially should know and understand their industry values.

• • •

A word of advice for my younger readers: Don't be complacent due to your youth. The one irreversible truth in life is that you will be old much longer than you will be young and you will get there much faster than you think. Pay close attention now and begin the habit of tracking your accomplishments and perfecting the ability to assert your value.

SOFT SKILLS ARE HARD TO COME BY

Notice in the section above that I used the term "value" and not "production." An employee can have an intangible value that you can't put your finger on but will be appreciated by an employer.

What I'm talking about are soft skills and not everyone has them. Just because you can't quantify your contributions to the organization in dollars and cents as easily as a sales person, you can describe other value you bring to the job. Perhaps it is your ability to work with people, the way you can schmooze (but not sell) potential customers in the lobby or your amazing ability to put people at ease in, say, a doctor's office.

It might be savings realized as a result of your knack for doing things more efficiently or your extensive knowledge and commonsense ability to blend new and old company systems that make you more valuable. Or maybe you go beyond your competency as a store manager and knock the ball out of the park as a customer favorite—the person people seek out when needing how-to advice.

These are intrinsic values that not everyone is capable of and with them, you significantly contribute to the overall mission and goals of a company.

So if you are one of those people who work their fingers to the bone on the non-revenue-generating side of the house, figure out what you do best to contribute and be able and prepared to say how your personal skills outside the job description make you invaluable to the company.

A WORD FOR REVENUE GENERATORS (AKA SALES PEOPLE)

In my career as a job search expert, rarely did I work with sales people because you inherently speak the language of achievement utilizing terms such as goal, quota and plan on a daily, weekly, monthly, quarterly and annual basis. Get my drift? That's a lot of accomplishments tallied, presented to supervisors and required to keep the job.

Nevertheless salespeople, it will pay off for you to begin tracking and retaining your accomplishments year over year in detail because at some point in time you are likely to move into management and I promise you will not be able to remember all that you are achieving right now. The information you deem important enough to collect at this point in your career will be invaluable to you later in your quest as you move up the corporate ladder.

Now that you know some of the ways you are valuable to your employer, it's time to prove it.

Chapter 5

Sourcing Your Accomplishments

Sourcing your accomplishments – a no brainer, right? Well, not necessarily. It depends on how much of your personal history you have available to you, how good your memory is and where you may be on your 40 year career trek.

If you are just out of college and trying to make the right impression to land that first job, accomplishments dating back to high school are acceptable. If you are heading toward the last five or 10 years of your career, you need highly visible, make-or-save-money accomplishments that express value beyond question.

In either case, however, the first stage of developing your Accomplishments Worksheet and Statement is to compile an exploratory list – just notes at this point about those things you have done that you are proud of. Don't worry about any kind of order or background details yet. Make an initial back-of-the-envelope-style list by using just a few words to remind you to flesh it out later or, if it all comes back to you now, then take the time and write it down.

As you begin to think about your accomplishments, it will help you to keep a pad and pen on your night stand. I guarantee that during this early process of creating your list, you will be drifting off to sleep and something will pop into your head—especially now that I have planted this seed in your brain.

Do not believe that you will not remember what you were thinking in the middle of the night when you wake up! Make a note of it right on the spot even if it is just a couple of words. When you get up in the morning you will glance at your pad and think, 'Oh, yeah! That!'

One more thing. During this exploratory phase, everything is significant. If you think it might have value for your list, it does. You can always toss it later.

There are two ways to track down past accomplishments: Your memory and other people's memories. Begin with your own by reviewing old performance reports. They are gold! (I hope you saved every one of them from everywhere you have ever worked. If you were - or are - in the military, you should have copies of every report ever generated on you.)

Next, look at previous resumes or curriculum vitae (CV) and any biographies you might have. Resumes are good for reminding you of that time you did something spectacular.

Are you of the age that you might still have old business planners about? Flick through them. I have found them to be an incredible source of former contacts and projects and events I was involved with.

Also, and this can be fun: Google yourself.

DETAIL

As your list grows, start adding detail behind each bullet. Tell a story. Nothing is more important at the time of an interview or a performance review than somebody asking you to tell them how you accomplished something and you being able to go into the specifics without ever breaking eye contact.

Never forget (this is important)

When someone asks you, "How did you do that?" what they are *really* asking is, "*Can you do that for me*?"

As you work through this process, it is not enough to just state an accomplishment as fact. You must also be credible in stating that which you achieved. Keep your audience in mind and write in a manner you know he or she will appreciate. Professionally impressing your immediate supervisor is your preliminary goal but always be thinking at least one step beyond your boss. At any time and for any number of reasons, your boss could leave the company at which time you will be positioned for the promotion.

To this end, structure your notes using language that implies how any accomplishment previously achieved can be replicated to the benefit of the company. Do this on paper now and you will naturally find yourself communicating in a similarly detailed fashion when the opportunity presents itself. Think of it as a soft-sales pitch or being matter-of-fact informative without the appearance of boasting.

• • •

There is an art to explaining how you accomplished something while withholding some of the details—especially with your immediate supervisor and management who may have-been-there and done that. If the situation allows, holding back the final 3 to 5 percent (or more) of how you accomplished something will prove to all parties involved that they need and recognize your value. And don't fool yourself: This is a management strategy that goes back for as long as managers have managed.

Depending on your age or position, you might not be comfortable with this view. I understand that. But no matter your rank or position, you would be wise to at least give this point some thought. Whether or not you decide to execute is up to you.

Regardless, strive to position yourself as irreplaceable—at least in management's view. I can't really advise much more on this except to return to the concept that you must know and be aware of the chemistry between you, your boss and your boss's boss, the culture of the business and how deep each member of the team might be involved in any project or process as to how much or how little information you can retain for your own benefit.

• • •

When adding details to an accomplishment, write down every aspect you can think of: The good, the bad and the ugly.

- Start with the Who, What, Where, When, Why and How of the project.
- Think in terms of the result. As you write, think of each achievement on your list as a short article. A

resulting net conclusion is required. More on this in the next chapter.

- As previously stated but worth repeating, keep your audience in mind at all times. This list is ABOUT you but it is not FOR you. It is for your supervisors.

- Ponder the details as if you were your own employer. How will a senior member accept this statement from *their* point of view? Did this achievement hit goals or show consistency of performance? Would that person view your statement as producing value based on what you are being paid?

- What types of predicaments did you encounter and how did you deal with them? This is a core principle of presenting valued accomplishments. Without problems who needs you? *Problems create opportunities.* Think hard and deep on those difficulties that someone without your specific skills and expertise may not have been able to overcome as efficiently or as effectively. How you achieved success is a crucial component of these stories.

- Was the project completed on-time and on-budget? If so, be prepared to speak to the details. If not, be prepared to explain why it did not. Some of your greatest accomplishments could be based on an event such as the need for you to take over the reins of an existing project from someone to salvage and re-stage.

- Was there a team member or members who did not perform as expected? How did you handle the situation? You don't have to name names but this sort of issue is an ideal place for you to point to your managerial skills.

As you make notes and flesh out your accomplishments, go for the WOW factor whenever possible. Show how you stand head and shoulders above the crowd. How you, and only you, are capable of doing the job really well and, by extension, are the person who should be considered for promotion over any other potential candidate.

Your goal when composing an accomplishment is to make yourself more compelling and more memorable than any of your coworkers. Rewrite until you get it right.

PERSONAL AND PROFESSIONAL

There are two types of accomplishments—professional and personal. For the purpose of business, the focus must be professional. However, if you are just starting out in your career, personal accomplishments related to those things you might have done in college or even in high school can have value.

● ● ●

If you are just starting out in your career, exploit this moment in time for all you can. You are a first-time job seeker only once in your life and as such you may be granted a wee bit of leeway at this time. However, after you land your first position, you are, from that moment forward, playing in the big leagues. Never again will you be able to sell yourself based on all those wonderful things you did in high school or college.

And on another note—if possible never leave a job until you have been promoted at least once. That promotion gives you something to talk about and a hiring manager much more reason to pay attention to you at your next interview.

• • •

Chapter 6

Who Are You Gonna Call?

By now, you have should have done all you can to track down accomplishments from your memory, performance reviews and resumes. The second, and most valuable, way to discover past accomplishments is through all the people you know—both personally and professionally. This is the 'heavy lifting' part of the process not because it is difficult but because it requires you to get on the phone and contact people you may or may not have remained in touch with. No worries. This is a great reason to reconnect.

I know that some of you will attempt this part of the process via email. I can tell you categorically that email *does not work*. People will respond, if they respond at all, not with accomplishments but rather with a general job recommendation. "Joe, you were a great employee" does not speak to achievement. That's a reference. With a phone call you can manage the conversation around what you really want to learn from them.

Another point in favor of making the call over sending an email is this: once you have sent an email and received a useless response, will you have the nerve to then call up that individual and press them for more information?

Even with that, I know that some of you won't believe me about the power of the live, in-person telephone contact. Here's a true story about that.

A woman called on me to help her move out of self-employment and back into a position that offered benefits—retirement benefits specifically. I asked her to begin the accomplishments process and even before she had paid me for my services—which at that point had been only about an hour of coaching—she had her old job back. And when I say old, I mean it.

She reached out to her former boss whom she had not spoken with in the eight years that she had been working for herself.

After her former boss learned that she was seeking accomplishments to find her way back into a corporate position, the boss told her that they had never been able to successfully replace her in the eight years she had been gone.

Then the boss asked if she would she like to come back to the national company where she had previously worked? She did.

Something similarly amazing happens so frequently to people who make the effort to personally contact friends, family, former employers, etc. that it no longer surprises me. The process works that well.

There is a long list of people you should contact in support of your accomplishment investigation.

Let's start with **FAMILY,** especially your mother. It's likely that you have told your mom everything good that has ever happened in your career or job. And moms remember everything good you have ever told them. No kidding. Moms are an amazing source of accomplishments and they are always eager to help!

If you have kids, ask them if they recall anything you've told them about work. Kids are a sponge who will recall stuff that you may not have considered such a big deal at the time.

Obviously ask your spouse or significant other. The truth is that you can probably acquire 30 percent or more of your accomplishments from just those members of your family who remember you bringing your work home with you.

FRIENDS –both on and outside the job—are good sources for pretty much the same reason as family. Close friends can be a wealth of information. Go back and try to get them to remember some of your wins.

SUPERVISORS are obviously a great and important source to discuss professional achievements with. They will especially remember the ones that made a positive impact on their own careers. Whether or not you want to discuss any of this with your current supervisor is something you need to ask yourself prior to taking any action. Once again I defer to the chemistry discussion. If your current supervisor might consider your crafting such a list as a threat to their own well-being on the job, then maybe you should skip him or her.

CO-WORKERS, not to be confused with on-the-job friends, particularly those you worked with in teams or shared office space with. Don't leave out anybody on your list even if they have moved on and you may not have stayed in touch with them. Like I said earlier, this could be the ideal way to reconnect. Not sure where they might be? Start with LinkedIn and/or Google them.

CLIENTS/CUSTOMERS are a great source for seeking accomplishment-worthy stories especially if you helped solve problems they were dealing with in their own businesses.

VENDORS are similar to clients and customers but in reverse. They may have provided you with service and support and/or materials to make a project come to fruition.

Think about those vendors and suppliers who have been there for you in the past and give them a ring.

ASSOCIATIONS can be valuable places to seek out information on previous achievements, particularly business associations. Check with those you meet with on a monthly or annual basis. They'll remember war stories you may have told over chicken dinners.

MILITARY, for those of you actively serving, live and work with an accomplishments mindset daily. I'm a veteran and I know every job in the military is directed toward a goal. Veterans and active duty military have access to their performance reports and should keep copies. Beyond that, reach out to former service members you worked with and after reconnecting, ask about those achievements of yours that were above and beyond the call.

An important side note: Military engagement, combat readiness and the training required to make that happen all fit (ironically) into the soft-skills aspect for detailing an accomplishment. Leadership, command, teamwork and team responsibility are highly admirable qualities that deserve mention and recognition in your accomplishments.

PROFESSORS AND TEACHERS can provide a lot of support for this cause. Every teacher and professor (assuming they remember you) is pleased to participate in this type of activity. They are motivated by your success because your success is theirs too. This applies to new and recent grads as well as to time-in-grade professionals.

COACHES. Are you, were you an athlete? Reach out to former coaches for stories of teamwork and the personal assistance you offered teammates during your playing days. This also applies to life, business and career coaches you may have worked with. It is their job to detail this sort of information.

CLERGY. Are you active in your church, synagogue or mosque? The same applies as it does in coaching. Religious leaders may be able to spark memories of events you participated in, from working with a fundraising committee to volunteering in the community.

VOLUNTEER/CHARITY. As I mentioned, most items on your list should be business and/or professional accomplishments but there is a place for past and current volunteer work. Call them. Reach out. Take notes. I'll come back to this when we talk about organizing your accomplishments for presentation.

THE QUESTION TO ASK

Now that you have a list of who you might approach, let's talk about how to initiate the conversation. When you connect with professional, non-family contacts, you don't need to conduct a complicated interview. In fact, there is only one question you need to ask—but stay with it until you get an answer:

When you and I worked together what difference did I make?
and/or
What impact did I have on the organization when we worked together?

All right – two questions that are actually two ways of asking the same thing. Note how easy it would be, if you email the question, for the person to respond with a generic job reference-type answer.

That is why I insist that you speak by telephone. On the phone, if you get the generic reference answer, you can say, "I appreciate that but what I am really looking for are some actual incidents, specific events or projects where we successfully worked together or maybe you remember something I did on my own that was noteworthy."

This exercise, although it takes a little time, is worth the effort. The fact is, *you did things*, probably more than you realize, that have made positive impacts on others' lives, business outcomes and futures. In addition, you have undoubtedly forgotten some outcomes or possibly never knew about them to begin with.

Our actions in life can be compared to a pebble being tossed into a pond that causes ripples to cross over to the far bank. These ripples, your actions, often go deeper and move farther than you know.

Let me illustrate with another true story.

I was conducting one of my full day job search workshops where I presented this Accomplishments Worksheet exercise. One candidate, Joe, was so taken with this idea that he decided to text it out while I was speaking.

He texted 10 people—nine former co-workers and his former boss—asking them what difference he might have made during the time they had worked together.

Joe's back story is that he had recently retired from a community bank in Texas. After a few months he determined that he wasn't cut out for retirement. He attended my workshop hoping to pick up some new tactics with the intention of putting himself back on the market.

In a flash, Joe got a text back from his former boss saying that he had "saved the bank."

What?!

During the next break, Joe ran out to call his former boss to ask him what the heck he was talking about.

At the time of Joe's "saving the bank," we were in a national recession and the Federal Deposit Insurance Corporation (FDIC) was running around the country shutting down and selling off under-capitalized banks. Joe's boss had been informed that his bank, with no way of acquiring additional funding to meet reserve requirements, was potentially in danger of being taken over by the agency.

At about the same time, Joe had pitched a new program and product. Joe's boss told him to run with it. Joe created the program, implemented and sold it to the public. It was an overwhelming success. Effectively, and without his knowing it, Joe had saved the bank.

So why didn't Joe know about this before now? His boss, hoping to avert the crisis, had never said a word about it to anyone for fear that morale would be shot and staff would jump ship. Then, after the situation was avoided he figured why bring it up at all?

The moral of the story for our purpose is this: Had Joe not asked his previous employer what impact he had made, he would never have known about this colossal accomplishment.

I don't expect you to find out that your efforts prevented a ship from sinking but, based on my experience, you may be surprised by what you learn.

Chapter 7

How To Craft A Compelling Accomplishment

Okay, by now you should have a detailed list of your accomplishments with lots of random—or not so random—notes on how you made a difference gathered from resumes, performance reviews and all those family members, supervisors, co-workers, clients, customers, vendors and others you spoke with, right? Good work! You might think you have too much information but you don't. For now, save everything you have collected.

So what's next? What are you supposed to do with all that amazing information about how terrific you are?

That's what this chapter is about. With my guidance, you are going to craft each accomplishment into a single captivating statement. Earlier I told you to seek the How, What, Where, When and Why for providing the back story to each accomplishment. Now, for the purpose of crafting individually compelling statements you will focus only on the What.

When you are done this assertion will be so persuasive that your employer cannot help but ask, "How did you do that?"

Let's get started.

Every good book, movie, TV show or song has a beginning, a middle and an end. So, too, does every accomplishment. The trick is to keep it simple but still tell a story so compelling it cannot be ignored, and that gives you the perfect opportunity to articulate your capabilities.

Here are those three components as they relate to the accomplishment narrative you will build:

Beginning = Statement of Accomplishment (what you did)

Middle = (will always be) "that resulted in" (or something similar)

End = Value Stated or Net Result (your accomplishment)

Here is what a great accomplishments statement using that three-part formula looks like: "Created a digital filing system that resulted in 300 man hours saved per week enabling the firm to save $6,240,000 annually."

WOW! No one, certainly no employer, hears a statement like that without asking a lot of questions and that is what creates your perfect opportunity to tastefully inform others about how good you are.

Maybe you think you haven't done anything as outstanding as that. Well, maybe, maybe not. The statement above is one person's real accomplishment but it wasn't anywhere near as evident as this when I first began working with her.

My client, a highly experienced paralegal, proudly told me she had "created a filing system" to which I answered, "So what?"

She got angry. I mean, really mad!

When she calmed down, she went on to tell me that I didn't understand. She had created a digital filing system out of files that had for years resided in boxes, metal filing cabinets, on microfiche and in film canisters that took up two entire floors of a downtown office building. She had successfully converted it into a digital masterpiece (my term, not hers).

"That's not what you said," I told her. "You said you created a filing system and to me (or anyone listening), a filing system could be as simple as lining some folders up in a file drawer. Not a big deal."

Sometimes it's too easy for any of us, maybe because our culture conditions us to not boast, to overlook the money punchline, as happened with my paralegal's example. In this exercise, humility is your enemy and you don't have me to pressure you, so look for what you do really well and maintain that focus.

Let's analyze the paralegal's finished accomplishment statement to see exactly how it breaks down.

Beginning ="Created a digital filing system"
This accomplishment opens with a simple statement of the *What* she did…
Middle = "that resulted in"
End = "300 man hours saved per week enabling the firm to save $6,240,000 annually."

…and concludes with a Value Statement.

Bam! She nailed it!

Inherent in that ending and a requirement for any accomplishment statement is a net result of some type. It can be revenue gained or saved, or a description of a process improvement resulting in a concluding statement such as "reduced turnover" or "enhanced inventory control."

In the paralegal's case, her digital filing system produced a huge time savings (and time is money) for the law firm and although it is left unsaid, no supervisor or employer would miss that it also demonstrates that she is capable of undertaking an enormous project and bringing it to a successful conclusion.

☑ RULE: No Statement is an Accomplishment until it has a Net Result!

Here is the exceedingly simple accomplishment statement formula:

(I was*) Responsible for _____that resulted in_____.

All you have to do is fill in the blanks. Remember, the first blank tells me *what you did.* The second blank tells me *how what you did added value to the organization.* A What statement with a Net Result.

And don't dismiss the middle phrase - "resulting in" or "resulted in." This phrase as close to business gold as there is – managers, owners and boards of directors thrive on results. Give it to them!

To bring home how important a well-crafted statement is, all you have to do is ask yourself which paralegal/filing clerk/project manager would you hire? The one who said, "I created a filing system" or the one who said, "I created a filing system that resulted in millions of dollars in savings?"

•   •   •

** **Note that I struck** "I was" from the formula sentence above. Never begin a professional statement with that personal pronoun in the first sentence. If an accomplishment must run on to a second sentence, you might use "I" in that sentence. (I suggest you try always to keep accomplishments to a single sentence.) Here is an example of a two-sentence statement.*
"Responsible for 49% of all sales resulting in $7,231,955 to the bottom line. I was able to achieve this level of revenue as a result of relentless pursuit of large scale, repeat users of the ABC product line."

•   •   •

ACCOMPLISHMENTS & TEAM

Yes, I know: There is no "I" in team. But what if one of your more significant accomplishments was a team effort; what if it took eight of you to _____? How should you express *team* in your accomplishment statement? The simple answer is: You don't.

Recruiters will tell you that although you worked with a team, you must point out your contributions to the success of the overall project as if you had done the deal by yourself.

This can be hard sometimes and you may not be comfortable doing so but a raise or a promotion is not going to a team — it is going to you. Or, rather, it will when you know how to express your contribution in a singular manner.

Of course, credit should always be given where credit is due. Except for now. Seriously. Never feel bad about promoting only yourself. Here is an example of a team member's contribution written in that one person's voice:

- *Responsible for 97% occupancy of the Acme Building due to diligent and consistent pursuit of a competing office complex's primary tenants. Able to relocate 3 tenants for a cumulative total of 320,000 net rentable square feet at an average rate of $23 per square foot resulting in $7,360,000 gross annual revenue.*

Having been in the commercial real estate business for several years, I can tell you categorically that no real estate deal is a solo achievement. It takes a lot of people moving in the same direction at the same time to accomplish the renovation and relocation of 300,000+ square feet.

Nevertheless, nowhere in my description of this achievement did I say or even imply that a team of any kind was involved. To a professional in the industry, there would be an unwritten understanding that you did not, in fact, accomplish this on your own and to state an accomplishment this way and in this manner is normal and acceptable.

If, however, you won the gold in an Olympic team sport, you may not be able to deny the team component. In the end it is up to you to decide how best to state any team-based accomplishments.

THE REST OF THE STORY

Earlier I asked you to do a detailed workup for each accomplishment, gathering information from old resumes, performance reports and all those telephone conversations from family to colleagues and former bosses. I also told you to include in your notes not only the good but the bad and ugly as well. There is a crucial reason.

After your employer or interviewer is stunned by your amazing three-part accomplishment sentence, he or she will have a lot of questions, some of them quite detailed. Here is how my paralegal would have explained and expanded on her digital filing accomplishment:

> *"This project took one year and a team of six, temporary, full-time employees to complete. I was*

responsible for the digital transference of all pa-
per and microfiche files accumulated by the law
firm over a period of decades.

Based on an average rate of $400 per man hour
(rate provided by CFO), I saved the firm $120,000
per week (based on an average of 300 man hours
of weekly access to the historical files by staff
x $400) or $6,240,000 ($120,000 x 52 weeks)
annually. This project came in on time and on
budget."

Undoubtedly, she would then be closely questioned on such matters as the amount of the budget allotted, how much was spent on temps, equipment, software, implementation, etc. She would be asked about what difficulties or snags she encountered and how she resolved those problems, turning the bad and the ugly into gold.

And that's how all the hard work you do with old resumes, performance reviews and telephone conversations pay off. You will already have reviewed your past successes, their details, obstacles and solutions so that when asked, you will have all the details at the tip of your tongue.

When you are as thoroughly prepared as this to recall every aspect of the project you are asked about you will, like my paralegal, be first in line for the promotion or job.

The Accomplishment Statement system works at every level of an organization. It makes no difference if your audience is your manager, the owner or the board of directors.

The power of an accomplishment is in its net-present value to your employer.

Read that statement again. Make this statement your accomplishment mantra. The power of an accomplishment, in the eyes of your manager or employer, is in the value you bring to your business unit or organization today!

Chapter 8

Accomplishments Trump Discrimination On The Job

No matter what you look like or how different you may be, whatever your age, race, ethnicity, gender, sexual orientation or any physical challenges you may have, if you can *make an employer money* or *save them money* you can get the job, earn the promotion or retain your position.

I'm not saying it is always easy or that discrimination is not a widespread issue. It is. There will always be employers who skirt equal opportunity laws and even disregard them. But in the end, it is revenue – the "make them money or save them money" mantra I keep harping on – that wins the day. And sometimes, it's your difference that gets you hired.

One example: I have a close friend who owned a very hip, avant-garde restaurant. Richard went out of his way to hire the most unconventional (for the purpose of this discussion think: discriminated against) wait and kitchen staff that he could find. These were good people who, for the most part, had been passed over by virtually all other employers. Letting it be known that his restaurant was a great place to work for those who needed a "real job" while trying to break into whatever field they were pursuing, Richard almost exclusively supported the local artistic community.

His staff had long hair, piercings, studs, dreads and probably more "ink" than most tattoo parlors have on their walls. Due to his support for those who were generally not even considered for traditional employment, Richard had a stable, colorful (in all aspects of the word) and loyal staff who enjoyed having a job that fit into their lifestyles. These employees represented value and made his business a success.

This wasn't charity on Richard's part—they made him money. The restaurant became a recognized fixture in the community. There *are* enlightened employers out there.

•   •   •

Although the remainder of this chapter, for the most part, addresses age discrimination, the advice is easily adaptable to whatever kind of discrimination you might face.

• • •

Unless you get rich while you're young and retire, age discrimination is an issue that most all workers will face at some point in some manner in their career. It may be hard for you who are just starting out to envision but take my word for it and begin working a plan now so that you can stay ahead of the game.

In my experience with mature job seekers over the past several years, too often men and women over the age of "ahem" were terminated not because they weren't doing a good job, not because they were not exceptionally capable but, in my view at least, because they didn't keep the powers-that-be informed of their value. When they came to me, and as I put them through the same exercises I've given you in this book, it became immediately apparent to me that they had a lot of talent, current knowledge and experience yet to share.

Unfortunately, and for too many reasons to get into here, it is too easy for senior management to decide they can replace $150,000-a-year-plus-bonuses-Bob with $70,000-a-year, 27-year-old MBA Sally. (And, to be clear, I'm not faulting go-getter Sally for landing the job!)

Bottom line: consider this a wake-up call. All of this plays into succession planning, accounting and how current management perceive your value. Keep your Accomplishments Inventory/Statement up to date—including the monetary value of those achievements—because people other than you are keeping track of your performance as the years go by.

MINIMIZING AGE IN ACCOMPLISHMENTS

Recall the accomplishment statement of my paralegal after we rewrote it within the format and compelling result:

"Created a filing system that resulted in 300 man hours saved per week
enabling the firm to save $6,240,000 annually."

Did you notice that there is no Where or How this accomplishment took place even though I required that she provide me with those details? This is by design. Did you also notice there is no When, that she did not say she created this filing system in 1999 or 2007 or 2015? That was by design also.

We also left out the name of the law firm for which she performed this miracle. The reasons for doing so vary and it is up to you to decide whether to mention the company by name. Here are some guidelines:

- If it is a great, name dropping-worthy corporation then by all means include it. Amazon? You bet! ABC Loan and Pawn? Maybe not. But even if unknown on a state or national level, if your company is a big-deal in the local economy and dropping that name would make an impact, use it.
- If the company for which you have listed an accomplishment no longer exists, there's no need to mention it unless, once again, it remains a recognized name with a positive history such as that of Compaq Computers which was acquired by Hewlett-Packard (HP).
- If the company is the one for whom you are currently employed then this is a no-brainer – name it and include the division or office you were/or are working with currently.

Again, choosing to use the name of the company or organization that you were employed by at the time of your accomplishment is up to you and I know I'm repeating myself but this is important: keep your audience in mind. Will the company name add value to your accomplishment? If not, save it for the in-person discussion.

ACCOMPLISHMENTS AND THE SENIOR WORKER

It doesn't matter if it has been a few years since you performed an accomplishment you want to list except for this caveat: Can you/would you still be capable of performing up to the standard you are claiming? Let me explain.

Some years ago, I was involved in a few online startups and I am confident I could still be a highly capable, contributing member of a startup today. But could I go on the road as a sound man for rock bands as I did in my 20's? Not a chance. I don't have the desire, let alone the energy, to load-in, sound check, mix and load-out an entire group's worth of equipment night after night. I would save those stories for friends, not an employer.

In deciding whether to mention an accomplishment that is a few years old, consider whether the current situation or company mission suggests a need for that kind of knowledge or expertise. You could, if you don't take time to think this through, actually do yourself professional damage by going back too far.

Remember my first rule: Never assume your boss knows exactly what you do or how you contribute? If a past accomplishment can help the company make money or save money today, do not assume your boss knows of significant triumphs in your not too distant past.

These are guidelines. I can't know your specific situation so you need to figure out whether to include older accomplishments on your own taking into consideration your boss's needs and the company position in the market.

DEGREE OR NO DEGREE

Education is another important consideration for older employees. When you started out, it's possible that a college degree wasn't required or that you started in the plant and due to the quality of your work, were promoted into management. Now, no matter how good you are, the lack of a college degree may be holding you back from moving further up the ladder or worse, could put you out on the street. As talented and successful as you have been, without the degree required for the job, are you working with a strike against you?

In these cases, it is even more important to take your personal accomplishments inventory and keep it up to date. Express your value. Defend your position, ability and livelihood by knowing what you've accomplished and not being shy (once again—appropriately) about what you have achieved and can continue to do.

For those of you who do quality work and are worth every dollar you are paid but do not have the degree now required of your position, I implore you to embrace the idea of not just an Accomplishments Statement but more — an Accomplishments Journal.

THE ACCOMPLISHMENTS JOURNAL

The idea of an Accomplishments Journal is nothing more than the compilation of a life's worth of accomplishments. An inventory of what you have done over your 40 years. As you engage in the practice of keeping an inventory of those things you have done well or of significant achievements you will eventually, year over year, begin to gather your personal work history. This is good.

Personally, I have accomplishments from years ago that I could replicate and would not be the least bit hesitant to present to a current employer. All things being equal and for the purpose of this discussion, the more current an accomplishment the better but there is no harm in presenting an older accomplishment relevant to the situation.

The Accomplishments Journal is an evergreen document. Your accomplishments potentially continue to have value over time as I expressed above and you can't - I mean, you *really* can't - begin to remember all that you have done or will do throughout your 40 years.

Establishing a journal now, regardless of your age, just makes it all that much easier to access valuable information now and into the future.

(And it might be an interesting document for you to leave behind, eh?)

Chapter 9

Format And Formal Presentation

Back in Chapter 3: *SOURCING YOUR ACCOMPLISH-MENTS*, there is a sample copy of Janet Best's Accomplishments Inventory. (I assume you know that Janet and her Accomplishments Statement are fictitious.)

There is also a copy of this same document at the back of the book in the Appendix for quick access. You may want to refer to this document while I discuss formatting. Note: You can also visit RickGillis.com to view a sample Accomplishment Statement.

Your Accomplishments Statement, in final presentation, is meant to be as formal and professionally attractive as a resume/CV or a cover letter and when presented, is designed to convey the professionalism of the person presenting it. You will get your supervisor's preliminary attention with formatting and then knock their socks off with content. So plan on spending a little time buffing out the margins, centering and, of course, no typos!

In the header, list your name, the title of the document, telephone number and email address. This is the minimum. Depending on where and to whom you are presenting this document, you may also want to include your current job title and location within the organization. You will know what is appropriate when the time comes.

Reviewing the sample document, take a look at Janet's header.

Janet titles her document "Statement of Professional Accomplishments" followed on the next line with her company's name, her corporate title, email address and direct phone number. You may find it reasonable to include a city and state and/or your postal mailing address.

Below the header, without a title or any explanation (none is necessary) Janet begins to list the accomplishments she considers the most valuable for her immediate supervisor and above to recognize. It doesn't matter that her supervisor may already know this information. Re-ringing a bell can have an impact.

Note that Janet lists her accomplishments using the Accomplishments Inventory formula: Accomplishment + "resulting in" + Value Statement. There are no company names, no time frame, none of the embellishments that you would find on a standard resume. Her statement is all about the What. Only. The How, When, Where, Why and Who (if appropriate) come when the question "Tell me more…" is asked.

She has organized them in the order she personally feels makes the best case for her efforts. This is something you need to do based on your job, what your supervisor expects of you and the inside knowledge you have from being in the environment.

Note that Janet's accomplishments are not numbered. This is by design so that no one accomplishment appears more important than any other. By using bullets instead of numbers you do not grant one accomplishment more value over another.

There is a double space between each of Janet's accomplishments, leaving a lot of white space so that this page reads easily. It also allows each accomplishment to stand on its own merits while inviting discussion. When your boss asks for more details, you have the perfect opportunity to have a focused discussion on your specific value to her.

In theory, there is no limit, no right number of accomplishments to include. In reality there *is* a protocol that is dictated by your company culture, your manager and you. You will know what the right number is. If you are in sales, two or more pages may be appropriate. Any other occupation will most likely be best served by presenting a single page. Stick with your intuition on this one.

• • •

Side note: I strongly suggest compiling your achievements into a journal but I do not recommend presenting this volume to management. View your journal as an archive of your professional history. In the event of a downsizing, you may want to produce the entire journal as validation for the value you have contributed over time and if current, will support your continued contributions.

The secondary value of your journal is providing you with all the highlights of your career when you decide to pen your biography!

• • •

As I have said several times throughout this book your goal is to see that decision makers are aware of the value you bring to the organization. All your work in gathering and writing your accomplishments, organizing them into a compelling list and creating a clean, clear presentation of them will get the job done.

HOW AND WHEN TO USE YOUR ACCOMPLISHMENTS

You've done all this work. You have a wonderful list of your highest and best accomplishments all laid out in a perfect order for the world to see. How are you going to use it?

If you are able to engage your boss casually over the water cooler you may be able to go about informing her about your latest, greatest accomplishment she may not be aware of. In my mind, a best-scenario application of this information would be truly informing, as opposed to boasting about something you have done recently that you are proud of and feel worthy of mentioning. Interestingly, it is a very real possibility that in the course of your career you may never actually present your formal written Accomplishments Statement to a supervisor. This assumes you are consistently able to seize the opportunity for one-on-one discussion. This possibility *does not* give you permission not to have a formal document prepared for other eventualities.

Here is a short list of those times when you may find it handy and necessary to have a printed Accomplishments Statement in hand.

- Performance reviews
- Requesting a raise or conducting a salary negotiation
- Contract negotiation for those of you who work by contract
- In defense of termination due to downsizing

This is by no means an all-inclusive list but you get the idea. Your Accomplishments Statement, besides building confidence, motivation and poise for you personally is a tool that can and should be applied on a consistent basis throughout your 40 years.

Chapter 10

Making The Accomplishments Case For Employers

The Brief: What if you were able to extract more value from your existing employees? Businesses continuously seek new methods of generating revenue. Implementing an accomplishments program companywide and using that source of information to coach your entire staff on how to soft-sell your product or service can help you accomplish this.

• • •

In Chapter One I asked, "Who do you have to promote you?" And the answer was simply: You.

Now I ask the same question with a change on emphasis,

Who does your company have to promote it?
Everyone on your payroll!

Depending on the size of your company you may at first think the answer would be your sales staff, marketing department, advertising agency, PR firm or even a social media group but are you letting your rank-and-file employees off the hook? Shouldn't everyone who works for you, regardless of their position, be prepared to professionally promote the company?

•   •   •

For the remainder of *PROMOTE!* I will discuss the concept of a company-wide accomplishments compilation program with a twofold objective: First, for you as a manager to acknowledge what your employees are accomplishing while on your payroll and second, to help create new revenues as a result of sharing those accomplishments with your entire staff for them to share with clientele. Expense to the company is minimal while the revenue generated could be significant.

Not too long ago I was approached by a friend who is a director of a national consulting firm. He was concerned because he felt too much money was being left on the table due to the inability of his staff of IT service providers to upsell clients when providing on-site service. (Remember the discussion on 'Analyticals' in Chapter 2?) As we discussed the issue further, he admitted that his on-site service providers would never be his best sales representatives. But then again, *maybe they should be*.

I do not know of any organization (although I will not go so far as to say that none exist) that takes the time to enlighten every employee *on a continuing basis* on the art of the soft-sell. In prospect, this may sound daunting but in practice, assuming you embrace the concepts that got you to this page in the book along with the very simple model that follows, it does not have to be difficult.

•   •   •

Service providers you send to your customers' places of business find themselves where no other person in your organization can. It comes with the territory of a service call.

Having been called in to take care of a problem, your employee has direct access to real decision makers—and I'm not talking about the purchasing agent. I'm talking about the people who actually perform the work. It makes no difference if we are talking about a data center, a refinery or a department store—there is always that core of people responsible for the hands-on implementation and oversight of operations

This is exactly the situation that my consultant buddy and I had been discussing over lunch. The question then became:

What if those service providers had current company accomplishments to share (Pitch? Soft-sell?) at the job site? All you would have to do would be certain that they had the most current information to share.

ENGAGEMENT & IMPLEMENTATION

How to accomplish this? (Pun intended.) This strategy calls for each employee to note five accomplishments monthly and submit them to their manager. That's it. Successfully engaging your staff relies in making the process simple and painless—and possibly profitable to participants should you decide to offer a monthly bonus or prize based on the value of those contributions.

But I digress.

What will your employees be taking note of? Those particulars have already been covered in chapters 1 through 9 but fundamentally, it comes down to what they have accomplished on the job since their previous report that they feel may be worthy of sharing with co-workers and clients.

METHODOLOGY

This process of acquiring accomplishments consists of ensuring everyone in your company produces a monthly list of those five things that they did the previous month that made an impact—any kind of impact—on the company. Process, efficiency, revenue, customer relations, savings, proving Einstein was wrong (just want to see if you are paying attention!)—anything that adds value to the organization no matter how incremental. Nothing is too mundane or too extraordinary to note. It all counts.

To illustrate, accomplishments can be as basic as achieving on time deliveries (Statement: "We had a 99.7% accuracy in on-time deliveries last month resulting in exceptional customer satisfaction and reduced complaints.") to writing a new, revenue generating app. A receptionist might include the moment she saved the day (and the deal) by turning a surly potential customer into an admirer of the company by doing little more than noting his disposition and offering up a cup of coffee and a cheerful good morning. If it made an impact it counts. All accomplishments should be in the voice and in line with the position of the person presenting it and should be considered accordingly. In other words, all of your employees are valuable. Give them their due. (Can you see a very simple model for a performance assessment tool emerging here?)

The overriding goal is to establish an employee mindset of watching for opportunities to make a difference to the success and profitability of the company. It is important to recognize that not everyone in every position will have had major wins or that they have to produce some miracle accomplishment each month. (Remember the payroll clerk's story in Chapter 4?)

SORTING ACCOMPLISHMENTS

So what do you do with a list of 5 accomplishments gathered from each of your employees monthly? The very first thing is to see that they are presented to their immediate supervisors as a short statement with a net result. (Keep in mind that if not presented with a net result it's not an accomplishment!) After that the possibilities for managing this action are pretty wide ranging. A small company may assign a single individual the responsibility of sorting and flagging stuff worthy of being shared with customers while larger organizations may assign each department, office, region, etc. the responsibility for the collection of this information. Also note that after 12 months each employee has compiled a list of 60 accomplishments. This is information that can be utilized in a myriad of ways.

These internal accomplishments are not generally meant to be shared with the public unless they are of a noteworthy and/or marketing caliber. The goal here is exactly the same for a company as it is for an individual: Individual employees want their supervisor to ask "How did you do that?" or "Tell me more." This is exactly the same response you want from clients and customers. The goal is to initiate the discussion that may lead to a sale or upsell.

Once determined to be worthy the best five accomplishments will then be shared with every employee in the company in a brief monthly text, email or internal press release—however you determine it best to disseminate this information. The only thing left to do is to encourage those road warriors, service providers and any other customer-facing employees to share (inform) online or in-person those accomplishments with an existing or potential customer.

Details and the 'rest of the story' employees may need can be made available on the company Intranet or perhaps posted on a public page available for public viewing if appropriate.

The idea that the sharing of accomplishments across the company could add to the bottom line is not a difficult stretch to make. Who's to say that the guy who goes out and services copiers couldn't have as big a month as a sales person at some point?

If you are interested in learning more about a simple and manageable performance assessment program based on this chapter contact RickGillis at rickgillis.com.

Addendum
"Yep, there's an app for that."

We all read books and articles and, with the best of intentions, think, 'Yeah! I'm gonna do that..." and then "that" gets away from us.

I know I'm asking a lot of your time when I suggest you source, quantify and then fully detail past accomplishments and then, from today forward, to keep a running list of your wins and all that you do on the job.

It was with this idea in mind that as I was completing PROMOTE! I went in search of accomplishment-based apps. And, not surprisingly, there are several for you to choose from. The ones that I reviewed prompt you via email or txt to make note of your daily achievements. In short, they are very simple to use and worth your effort.

I'm not going to promote (pun intended) any of them but I do recommend that you go to your app store and search the term "accomplishments" and find one that best suits your needs to make this process easy for you.

Thank You Very Much

Ronni Bennett/Editor for editing PROMOTE!, our fourth book together

Dayna Steele/Author/Speaker for writing a Foreword that Rocks

Gargi Kundu/Artist/Designer for her patience, eye and style

Alisa Murray/Photographer for her mastery with light and a lens

About the Author

Rick has been called the 'Job Search Mechanic.' This is because Rick Gillis truly understands and explains the mechanics of successfully navigating job search technology, in particular resume-filtering software—the number one obstacle for most job seekers. (To learn more visit RickGillis.com and click on the JOB! tab.)

Similarly, Rick is comfortable being the 'Accomplishments Mechanic' due to his expertise in teaching people the process of sourcing and stating their personal 'commercial' value. This book came about as a result of working with thousands of job seekers across the US and other countries. All that effort has now been translated into helping anyone who holds a job make the very most of it.

Rick aggressively promotes the concept that everyone should be recognized and well rewarded for their knowledge, skills and expertise on the job. And he believes if this is not the case then perhaps it's time for the employee to take the initiative to make it happen. Although this idea resonates with both men and women Rick especially promotes this message to women. During his years coaching women in their job search he found that virtually all of them were nervous about or simply would not negotiate salary. He insisted that his female clients negotiate not just for the money but also to establish themselves as a force to be reckoned with and earn the respect of the men they would work for and with. In nearly every case his clients were successful in this endeavor.

•   •   •

A pioneer of 21st century job search and a key player in launching the first job board serving the greater Houston, TX, USA area, Rick, has been noted & quoted regarding his three-step job search process in The Wall Street Journal, Forbes.com, The Houston Chronicle, CIO.com, ComputerWorld, BlackEnterprise, DallasNews, USATodayCollege, San Francisco Chronicle, HerCampus, and HuffingtonPost to name just a few publications and sites. Rick has been heard on NPR, PBS and countless radio stations across the US, Canada, the Caribbean and even Australia. Rick has appeared on television nationally; produced and hosted an employment-based cable TV show in Houston as well as hosting Rick Gillis Employment Radio in the Houston & Dallas markets.

Passionate about his work and wanting to share his knowledge with others, Rick appears across the country speaking to corporations, associations, networking groups, and college audiences. High energy, entertaining, focused, actionable, motivating and on-point are the terms most often used to describe Rick's live presentations.

For more information visit RickGillis.com.

Janet Best
Statement of Professional Accomplishments
Giant Company, Inc. / Southeast US Regional VP

email@GiantCompanyWebsite.com   123.456.7890

- Completed special assignments on inventory phase-outs, unallocated materials, and obsolete inventory resulting in savings to the company of $1,500,000.

- Improved operation scores for district to 90% from 82% in prior years as a result of group and individual coaching of district front line employees.

- Delivered a 12% profit increase over prior regional management by establishing new institutional accounts resulting in $6,000,000 of new revenue.

- Successfully trained tri-state team of over 800 managers, sales reps, technicians, and support staff on key company programs which resulted in improving service levels by 10%, improved operations processes and increased customer satisfaction.

- Repair center team ranked No. 1 in the country by J.D. Power & Associates. Achieved this level of customer satisfaction with the active involvement of all team members contributing to the plan.

- Improved past due performance of vendors by implementing a daily expedite program. Result: Logistics performance improved 43% compared to past output; past due orders reduced to 6% within 5 months.

- Led nation with an 18% improvement of sales in electronics by training store personnel on educating the customer on product functionality and reliability.

- Performed annual performance reviews and facilitated employees' creation of individual development plans which led to increased employee satisfaction and motivation by 15% over previous management team.

- Managed direct reports of up to 40 associates which included hiring, training, evaluating, coaching and transitioning employees. Turnover rates decreased 34% over previous management team.

- Improved accuracy of $10,000,000 spare parts inventory by 11% within 6 months after initiating a cycle count program.

- Designed a new expediting procedure that resulted in increased customer satisfaction and on-time customer deliveries by 28% within 4 months.

NOTES

NOTES

NOTES

NOTES